D0922283

Usborne Phonics Readers
Ted's shed

Phil Roxbee Cox

Illustrated by Stephen Cartwright

Edited by Jenny Tyler

Language consultant: Marlynne Grant
BSc, CertEd, MEdPsych, PhD, AFBPs, CPsychol

There is a little yellow duck to find on every page.

First published in 2006 by Usborne Publishing Ltd., Usborne House, 83-85 Saffron Hill, London EC1N 8RT, England. www.usborne.com
Copyright © 2006, 2001 Usborne Publishing Ltd.

Meet Ted. Ted likes red.

Even Ted's shed is a red shed.

Today, Ted's bed goes into the shed.

"What are you doing, Ted?" asks Fred.

"Wait and see," says Ted.

Up on his stool, Ted gets down his tools.

He puts in a paw,
and pulls out
a saw.

It's time to start sawing.

Ted looks at his drawing.

Ted saws into a big, round log.

"What are you up to?"
asks Pup the dog.

"Wait and see," says Ted.

He saws off a big, round slice.
"This wood is good. This slice is nice."

Now Ted saws off slice after slice.

Look who's watching – a pair of mice!

Next, Ted hunts for his jar of nails.

Look, the mice have the nails in their tails!

The jar
is empty...

...apart from
a snail.

Ted and his team work on in the sun.

They huff...

...and they puff...

...but it's lots of fun!

Fred and Pup ask, "What's this all about?"

"Just wait and see!" the others shout.

Did you spot Ted's clever plan?

His red shed is now a caravan!